Planes, Trains and Cars

Simon Abbott

Ticktock

HEAVY LOAD

Wonderful Wheels

There are lots of ways to get from A to B. Scooting or skateboarding cycling or roaring on a motorbike. Which do you like?

Ladies first! Make way!

Nice wheels, mate!

Early **scooters** were made by strapping roller skates to a wooden board.

Moder **scooters** ar far more hi-tec and can even be use to perform trick

In the 1880s when **bicycles** became popular, women swapped long skirts for bloomers so they could cycle too.

That doesn't look quite right?

'Chopper' **motorbikes** are modified by riders, who 'chop' them and put them back together. Cool!

The loudest **motorbike** audio system ever made is noisier than a jet plane!

In 2006 a man travelled across Australia on a **skateboard**, covering 3,618 miles in just over five months.

BMXs are used for stunts and tricks - even a triple backflip!

Weeeeee!

Roller skates were invented in 1760. It took a hundred years for them to be improved so skaters could stop and turn.

ONE WAY

Ralph Dadswell rode a **tricycle** from London to Edinburgh in 19 hours, 27 minutes. By car it takes about seven hours.

Zzzzzz

Penny farthings had enormous front wheels - some were as tall as a ten-year-old boy. It was a long way to fall if you crashed!

On the Road

Cars come in all shapes and sizes. Some are little, some are long, some are fast and some are slow. Unless there's a traffic jam, then everyone comes to a stop!

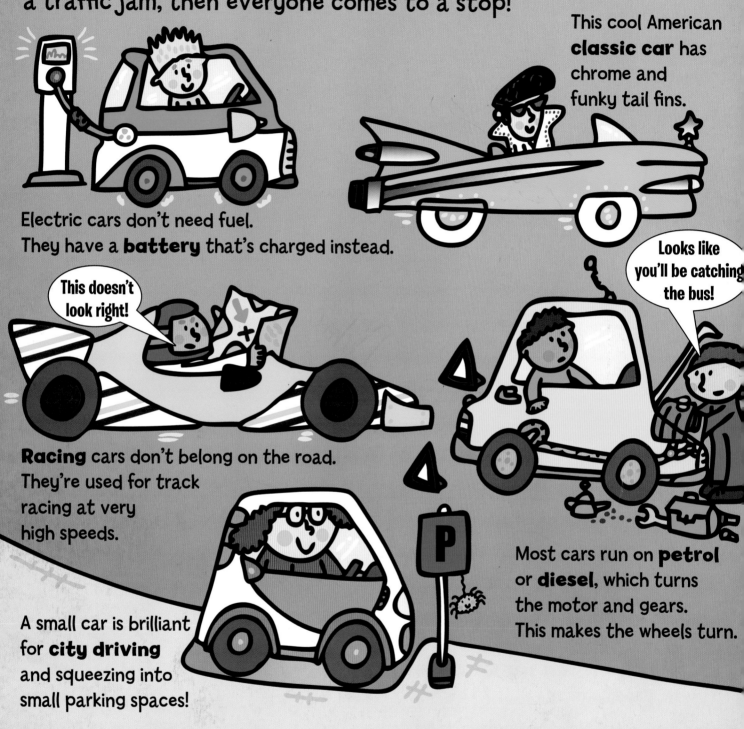

Electric cars don't need fuel. They have a **battery** that's charged instead.

This cool American **classic car** has chrome and funky tail fins.

This doesn't look right!

Looks like you'll be catching the bus!

Racing cars don't belong on the road. They're used for track racing at very high speeds.

A small car is brilliant for **city driving** and squeezing into small parking spaces!

Most cars run on **petrol** or **diesel**, which turns the motor and gears. This makes the wheels turn.

FUN FACTS

Did You Know? There are more than **one billion** cars on the world's roads.

Ready?

Stop! Go! The first **traffic light** was used in 1914 and was operated by a man in a booth!

Stretch **limos** are popular for parties and proms.

SUVs have plenty of **space** for passengers and luggage.

Are we there yet? Are we there yet?

Get a move on!

One needs to put one's foot down!

Drat! I've got a flat!

In Britain, **early cars** had to have a man walking in front of them waving a flag. They could only travel at 2 mph (3.2 km/h) in town!

Did You Know?
Early cars had no **fuel gauges.**

WOW!

Phew!

Strange...but true!
The very first cars were **steam-powered!**

All in a Day's Work

There are different vehicles for different jobs, whether it's mending roads, moving loads, delivering parcels or even new cars.

If you order something online it will be sent to you in a **delivery van**.

Oh, very funny

Backhoe loaders, or diggers, have an arm at the back with a bucket for digging, and a large shovel on the front. They weigh more than a male African elephant.

Refuse trucks pick up rubbish and recycling.

Fancy a banana milkshake?

A **milk tanker** can carry enough milk to fill 20,000 one litre bottles.

Lorries move things from place to place. They carry everything from food to clothes, furniture and books.

FUN FACTS

Did You Know?
A British man has collected 137 **traffic cones** - each has a different design.

In Canada, brave truckers drive huge lorries along ice roads made on frozen lakes, taking supplies to isolated towns.

You me

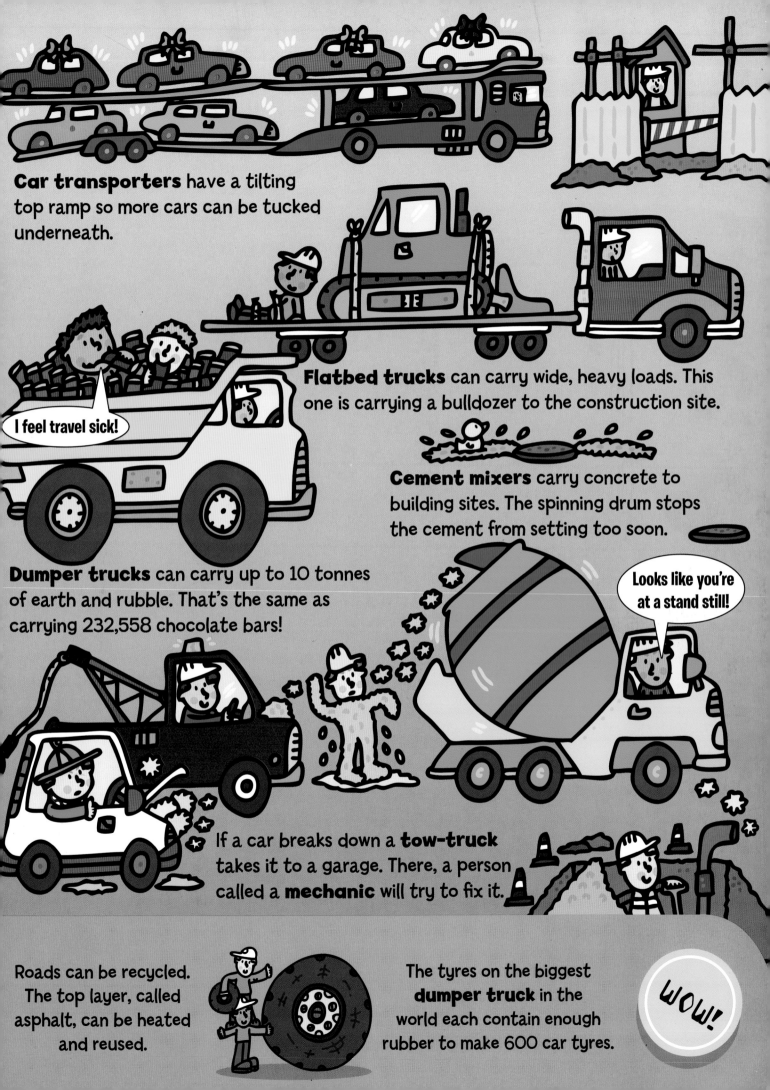

Car transporters have a tilting top ramp so more cars can be tucked underneath.

Flatbed trucks can carry wide, heavy loads. This one is carrying a bulldozer to the construction site.

I feel travel sick!

Cement mixers carry concrete to building sites. The spinning drum stops the cement from setting too soon.

Dumper trucks can carry up to 10 tonnes of earth and rubble. That's the same as carrying 232,558 chocolate bars!

Looks like you're at a stand still!

If a car breaks down a **tow-truck** takes it to a garage. There, a person called a **mechanic** will try to fix it.

Roads can be recycled. The top layer, called asphalt, can be heated and reused.

The tyres on the biggest **dumper truck** in the world each contain enough rubber to make 600 car tyres.

WOW!

All Aboard

Whether you're touring in a caravan or city sight-seeing in a bus it's great to be on holiday!

I can't find my passport!

Two British men travelled in a **double decker bus** through 18 countries in a record-breaking bus journey that took 13 months!

Grrrrrrr

Pardon me!

Sorry!

Excuse me!

I do apologise!

After you!

In Poland in 2011, 229 people crammed onto a **bus** for a record-breaking one-minute journey!

Follow that cab!

We should have said 'Neigh'.

SIGHTS of LONDON

In London, **black-cab** drivers must remember 25,000 streets and 20,000 landmarks and pass tests before they can start driving.

A horse-drawn carriage moves at about the same speed as a person jogging.

France's **TGV** train reached speeds of 357.2 mph – that's almost three times as fast as the top speed reached by a steam train!

The fastest **steam train**, Mallard, with a top speed of 126 miles per hour, has held the world record for more than 70 years.

Faster! Faster!

Don't even think about it!

More than seven million people use Tokyo's **subway trains** every day. At rush hour, staff push people into the carriages.

Did You Know?
A chilly train line in Tibet uses hot water in the toilets, to stop them freezing solid!

Japan's **Maglev** trains float 1 centimetre above the tracks.

WOW!

A Spanish man pulled a train for 10 metres, using his beard!

At the Airport

Last call for passengers to gate 16... But will you jet off on a jumbo jet, a double decker jet or a helicopter?

The **Airbus A-380** holds 4,429 times as much fuel as a family car.

The 747-8 jumbo jet is as wide as about 35 cars!

Airport buses take passengers from planes to the airport building. They can carry around 134 passengers.

Movie star on the move!

In one minute, an airport **fire engine** can pump out enough water to fill nearly 90 baths.

Flying High!

From hot air balloons to gliders, airships to bi-planes, there are plenty of other ways to fly, besides a jumbo jet...

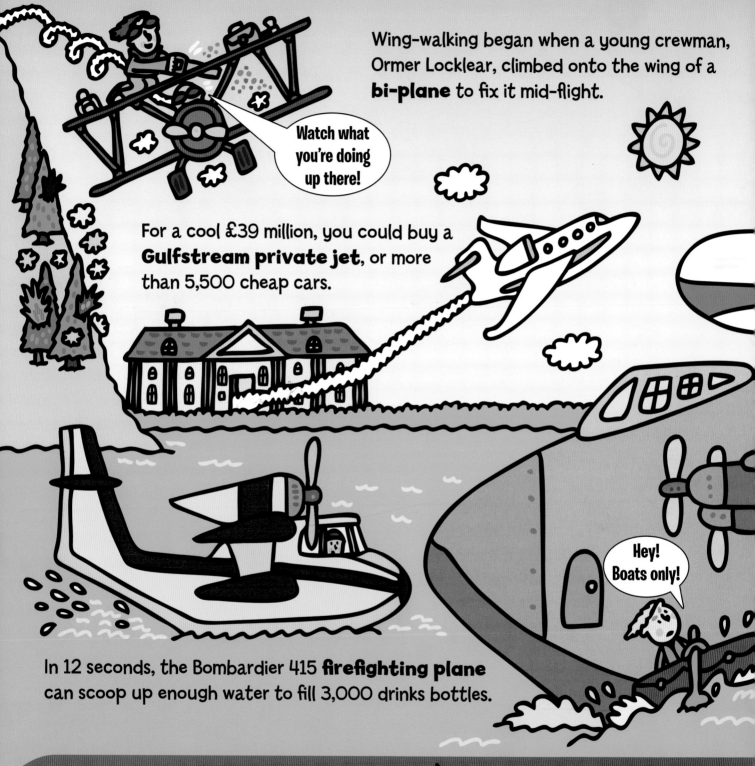

Wing-walking began when a young crewman, Ormer Locklear, climbed onto the wing of a **bi-plane** to fix it mid-flight.

Watch what you're doing up there!

For a cool £39 million, you could buy a **Gulfstream private jet**, or more than 5,500 cheap cars.

Hey! Boats only!

In 12 seconds, the Bombardier 415 **firefighting plane** can scoop up enough water to fill 3,000 drinks bottles.

FUN FACTS

Did You Know?
Humans first took to the skies in the **hot air balloon**, which was invented in 1783 by the Montgolfier brothers.

Concorde flew at twice the speed of sound. It could fly from London to New York in just three hours.

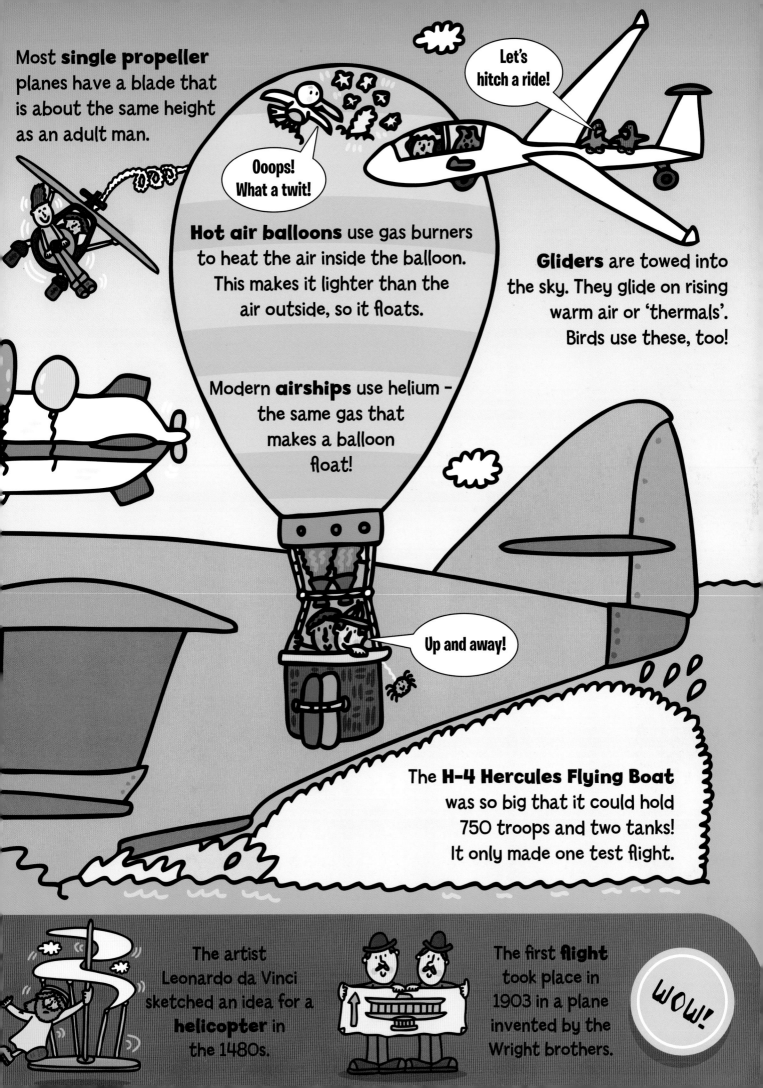

Setting Sail

Wild weather and mountainous waves are no problem for a sailor! Raise the anchor, it's time to set sail for an adventure!

Phew! Made it!

Fish fingers, anyone?

Smaller fishing boats, called **trawlers**, sail for weeks at a time. Many have freezers on board to keep their catch fresh!

Super aircraft carriers have a deck area as big as 97 tennis courts. They can carry more than 80 planes and helicopters.

Drop anchor!

One of the world's largest oil tankers, 'Seawise Giant' had an anchor that weighed as much as 567 men.

Watch out!

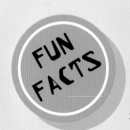

FUN FACTS

Did You Know?
In Australia, 145 water-skiers were towed by a single **speedboat**.

Whoops! Bit heavy on the brake!

One of the world's most expensive **yachts** contains solid gold toilets.

What's Inside?

Have you ever wondered what's inside a plane? Let's take a peek inside and find out what's in a jet.

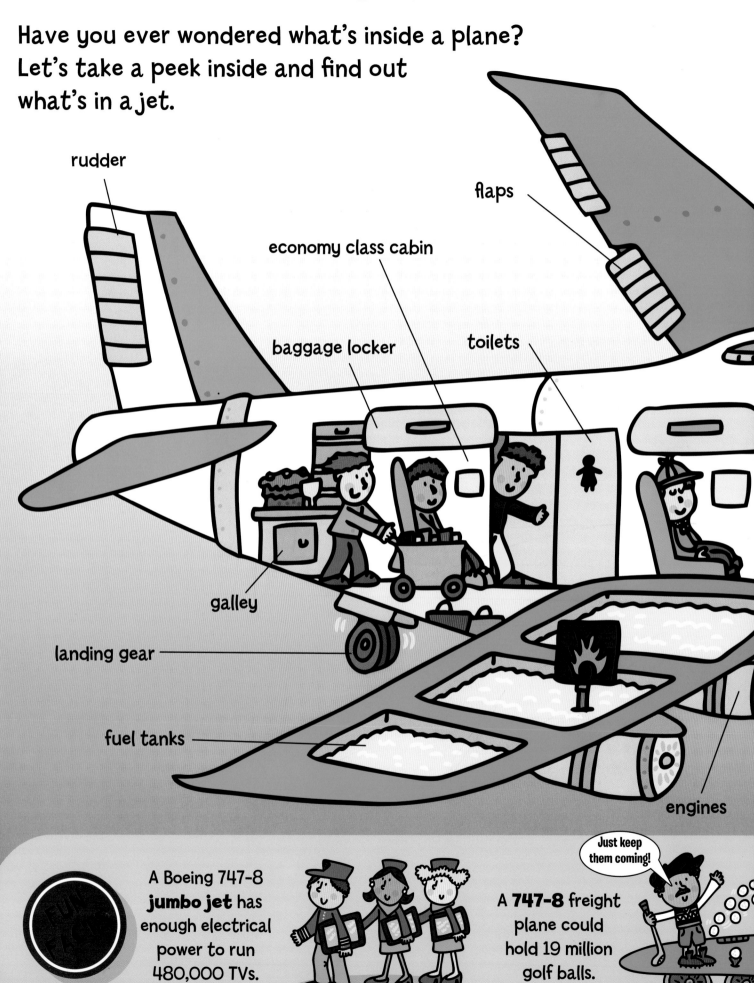

rudder

flaps

economy class cabin

baggage locker

toilets

galley

landing gear

fuel tanks

engines

A Boeing 747-8 **jumbo jet** has enough electrical power to run 480,000 TVs.

A **747-8** freight plane could hold 19 million golf balls.

Just keep them coming!

Jet Engine

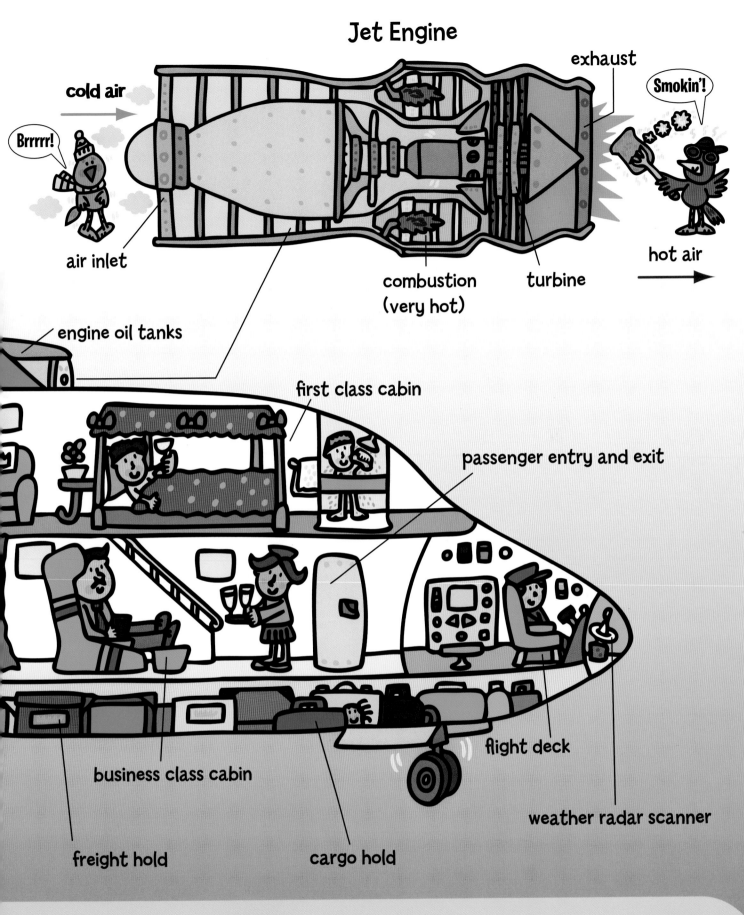

exhaust

Smokin'!

cold air

Brrrrr!

air inlet

combustion
(very hot)

turbine

hot air

engine oil tanks

first class cabin

passenger entry and exit

business class cabin

flight deck

weather radar scanner

freight hold

cargo hold

On take-off, a third
of the super jet liner
Airbus A-380's
weight is fuel.

The blast from a
jet engine
is powerful enough
to flip a car over.

Watch it!

WOW!

How Does it Work?

Ever wondered what makes a car work?
Let's take a look under the bonnet and find out more!

The **dashboard** tells the driver how fast he is driving and if there is a problem with the engine.

The **steering wheel** allows the driver to turn the car left or right.

Oil keeps the engine cool and parts working smoothly.

The **foot pedals** let the driver speed up, slow down and change gear.

Waste gas is pumped out of the **exhaust**.

The **fuel tank** holds petrol or diesel to power the engine.

The **handbrake** is used when the car is parked, to stop it rolling.

The driver uses the **gear stick** to change the speed and power of the engine.

The **battery** makes a spark when the engine is turned on to make the fuel burn.

FUN FACTS

The Peel 50 is the **smallest** car in production. It weighs less than an average man!

TINY 1

An American man built a **toilet car** using two loos. It comes complete with six loo rolls!